African Peoples of the Americas

From slavery to civil rights

Ron Field

Head of History

Cotswold School

CAMBRIDGE
UNIVERSITY PRESS

Published by the Press Syndicate of the University of Cambridge
The Pitt Building, Trumpington Street, Cambridge CB2 1RP
40 West 20th Street, New York, NY 10011–4211, USA
10 Stamford Road, Oakleigh, Melbourne 3166, Australia

First published 1995

Printed in Great Britain at the University Press, Cambridge

A catalogue record for this book is available from the British Library

Field, Ron
African peoples of the Americas from slavery to civil rights / Ron Field
            p.   cm. (Cambridge history programme. Key stage 3)
Includes index.
1. Blacks – America – History. 2. Afro-Americans – History.
I. Title. II. Series.
E29.N3F54   1995
970.004'96 – dc20 94 - 5375 CIP

The text in this book uses the terms 'black' or 'African' peoples when referring to those of African descent. However, the sources provided sometimes contain words used at the time. Often these words were used to offend or degrade people, but are retained in these pages as they tell us something about the ideas and feelings of those in the past.

Notice to teachers
Many of the sources in this text have been adapted or abridged from the original

ISBN 0 521 45911 7   paperback

Cover illustration: 'The attack on Fort Wagner by the 54th Massachusetts, 1863' from a series of lithographs published by Kurz and Allison c. 1880, Peter Newark's Military Pictures/Peter Newark's Western Americana

Picture research by Callie Kendall

Text illustrations by Nick Asher, Gerry Ball and Chris Molan

Acknowledgements
5t, Werner Forman Archive (British Museum); 5tr, Werner Forman Archive (Museum of Mankind, London); 5l, 6, 8t, 9c, 16, 20, 24, 25, 26, 29, 30t, 32t, 33t, 48, 49, 50l, 59, The Granger Collection, New York; 5br, copyright British Museum; 7, British Library, London/Bridgeman Art Library, London; 8b, 10, 14b, Hull City Museums & Art Galleries; 9t, City of Bristol Museum & Art Gallery/Bridgeman Art Library; 9b, courtesy of Peabody Essex Museum, Salem, Massachusetts (MB 405)/photo by Mark Sexton; 15b, 17, 21, John Judkyn Memorial; 13, Illustrated London News Picture Library; 14r, The Bodleian Library, University of Oxford (*Harper's Weekly*, 30 January 1864); 15t, The Slave Market by Friedrich Schulz (1823-75), Hirshhorn Museum, Washington, D.C./Bridgeman Art Library, London; 18, The Western Reserve Historical Society, Cleveland, Ohio; 30b, The Bodleian Library, University of Oxford (210.c.341, frontispiece); 31, courtesy of the National Portrait Gallery, London; 32b, Massachusetts Historical Society; 33b, 36t, 48, 51, 62r, Range Pictures/The Bettmann Archive; 38, *Harper's Weekly*, 10 May 1862; 39, *Harper's Weekly*, 5 November 1864; 40, 42, 43, Massachusetts Commandery Military Order of the Loyal Legion and the U.S. Army Military History Institute/photo: Jim Enos; 44, *Frank Leslie's Illustrated Newspaper*, 1862; 45, The Bodleian Library, University of Oxford (*Harper's Weekly*, 18 March 1865, [R.H.] 300.263.t.1/9, page 165); 50r, Franklin D. Roosevelt Library, Hyde Park, New York; 54r, The Denver Public Library, Western History Department; 55, courtesy Frederic Remington Art Museum, Ogdensburg, New York; 54l, courtesy of the Texas Memorial Museum, acc. no. 160-2; 61, Burt Glinn/Magnum; 62l, Popperfoto; 63l, Associated Press; 63r, Reuters/The Bettmann Archive

Contents

INTRODUCTION:

The African past

Timbuktu

GHANA

MALI SONGHAY Gao

Jenne

River Niger

BENIN

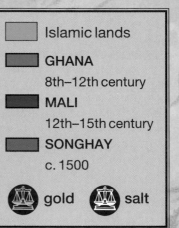

	Islamic lands
	GHANA 8th–12th century
	MALI 12th–15th century
	SONGHAY c. 1500
gold	salt

In the 16th and 17th centuries, Europeans thought that Africans were inferior and uncivilised, and as a result they felt justified in enslaving them. In fact, great civilisations had existed in Africa for hundreds of years. Muslim empires had long been established in North Africa. Between the 11th and the 16th centuries, Islam spread south. Muslim traders often made the dangerous journey south across the Sahara. They took luxury goods, salt and eventually firearms to exchange for gold, leatherwork and slaves.

By the middle of this period the economy of western Europe depended on African gold. While western Europe was in decline because of the effects of disease and war, great states like Ghana, Mali, Songhay and Benin flourished under a succession of powerful rulers. Renowned for their wealth and civilisation, their great cities like Timbuktu were centres of learning and art.

Source A

Arab scholar Abdullah Bekri describes the empire of Ghana in AD 1067, a year after William of Normandy conquered England:

> Tenkaminen, the king of Ghana, can put two hundred thousand warriors in the field. In court, he sits in a pavilion around which stand ten pages holding shields and gold-mounted swords, and on his right hand are the sons of the princes of his empire, splendidly clad and with gold plaited into their hair.

Source B

The rich trading city of Timbuktu, drawn (above) and described by early French travellers.

> Here are shops of craftsmen and hither do the Barbary merchants bring cloth of Europe. The inhabitants are exceeding rich. Here are great store of doctors, judges, priests, and other learned and hither are brought manuscripts or written books.

Source C
A necklace of twisted gold wire from Ghana.

Source D
A 16th-century bronze carving from Benin.

Source E
A 15th-century bronze plaque showing the emperor and princes of the highly civilised Benin Empire of Africa.

5

Black cargoes

In the 16th century white Europeans began taking large numbers of Africans to America as slaves.

Why did this process of slavery begin and how did it operate?

The idea of slavery is a very old one. The Pharaohs of ancient Egypt used slave labour to build the pyramids. The economy of ancient Greece and the might of the Roman Empire depended on millions of slaves. Slavery existed in Europe throughout the Middle Ages and there was a trade in African slaves in 15th-century Spain.

The Spanish colonisation of the Americas during the 16th century required hard physical work in order to clear woodland, cultivate and process crops, mine for mineral wealth, and build homesteads. Having gone to the New World to live like gentlemen, the Spanish forced the native people of the Americas, such as the Caribs of the Caribbean islands and the Incas of South America, to work for them under very harsh conditions. Exposed to new and fatal diseases carried across the Atlantic by Europeans, such as measles and smallpox, these native peoples died in their millions. By the early 16th century the Spanish needed an alternative source of labour for their colonies in the New World.

Source A

A modern history book, published in 1963, explains how black slaves were first brought to America:

Bartolome de Las Casas [a Spanish priest living in Haiti] stood before the throne of Charles V and implored him to spare the last of the Indians. Las Casas realised that there must be labour to work the plantations and the mines, but he had an excellent solution. Already a considerable number of Negro slaves had been brought to Haiti: they seemed happy and were hard workers. As an act of mercy toward the Indians, Las Casas begged his majesty to import other Negroes. In 1517 Charles granted one of his favourite courtiers a patent which entitled him to ship four thousand Negroes to the West Indian colonies. This was the beginning of the famous *Asiento*, an import licence which carried with it the privilege of controlling the slave traffic to the Spanish dominion in the New World.

The Granger Collection, New York

Source B
The Incas of South America being forced to carry gold for the Spanish conquistadores, 1590.

Source C

Slaves harvesting sugar cane in Antigua, 1823.

The growth of the slave trade

Slavery had existed in Africa, as in other parts of the world, from the earliest times. In the 15th century Portuguese explorers moved down the west coast of Africa establishing trading stations and building fortresses to protect the possessions they had seized. By the end of the century they were importing 10,000 African slaves into Lisbon every year. Many of the slaves were put to work on the Portuguese sugar plantations in Madeira and elsewhere.

In the early years of colonisation, the Spanish and Portuguese settlers in Central and South America used a relatively small number of African slaves as domestic servants and farm labourers. From the beginning of the 16th century an increasing number of African people were brought to work on sugar plantations in the Caribbean, Brazil and Mexico. During the next three centuries a massive expansion of slavery took place as the Portuguese and Spanish established their control of the New World and exploited the wealth of its natural resources.

Most of these enslaved people were not kidnapped by white traders but bought from African slave dealers. Large states, controlled by powerful African political and military rulers, were being set up in Africa at this time. Some of the people bought by the Europeans had been enslaved for debt and others as a punishment for crime but the great majority had been captured during fighting between warring African groups. The Europeans traded guns with African leaders and in return demanded slaves.

Source D
Sir John Hawkins, father of the English slave trade.

ATLANTIC OCEAN

Sugar, rum, tobacco, cotton exchanged for slaves

NORTH AMERICA

The triangular trade

THE SEA CAPTAIN, Sir John Hawkins, was responsible for beginning the English involvement in the slave trade. In 1562, he set sail from England for the west coast of Africa with a cargo of cloth and other valuables. In Africa he traded these goods for slaves, which he took across the Atlantic to the Caribbean. There he exchanged the slaves for sugar, silver and leather, which he then took back to England. This system became known as the 'triangular trade' and other European countries such as France and the Netherlands followed his example. Although the English did not have the *Asiento*, or licence, Hawkins made three more voyages along this route between 1562 and 1568. The trade, encouraged by Queen Elizabeth, was extremely profitable to the English, who became the biggest slave traders.

WEST INDIES

Slaves 'Middle Passage' 2-month voyage

Source E
A detail from a plan of a ship from Liverpool called the Brookes showing how slaves were carried on board. Men were loaded towards the bow (the front), boys in the centre, and women aft (the back, or stern, of the ship).

SOUTH AMERICA

Source F
Bristol Docks and Quay, early 18th century.

BRITAIN

The triangular trade brought death and appalling hardship to millions of captured Africans. Slaves were collected and kept in dungeons in European-built forts along the coast of West Africa awaiting shipment. European ships' captains went ashore and did business with African chiefs or traders, and herded their human cargo onto overcrowded sailing vessels. Then came the 'Middle Passage', or voyage across the Atlantic Ocean, with its dreadful death-rate. Between 1680 and 1688, for example, the British Royal African Company lost nearly a quarter of all slaves shipped from Africa. The slaves were shackled in pairs with leg-irons. They were branded with a red-hot iron, like cattle, to show who owned them; their heads were shaved and their clothes taken away.

Source G
A 16th-century engraving of the slave castle at Elmina on the west coast of Africa.

WEST AFRICA

Goods to trade for slaves

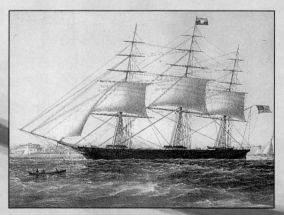

Source H
The American clipper Nightingale, known as the 'prince of the slavers'.

9

Source I

Slave merchants on the coast of Africa, painted by François-Auguste Biard in 1832.

• What similarities can you find between the scene in this painting and the description in Source J below?

Source J

Ottobah Cugoano was sold into slavery in the West Indies. Freed and taken to England, he published his *Thoughts and Sentiments* in 1787:

I saw many of my miserable countrymen chained two and two, some handcuffed, and some with their hands tied behind. We were conducted along by a guard, and when we arrived at the castle, I asked my guide what I was brought here for. He told me that I was to learn the ways of the white-faced people. I saw him take a gun, a piece of cloth, and some lead in exchange for me, and he went off. This made me cry bitterly, but I was soon conducted to a prison where I heard the groans and cries of my fellow-captives. When we were put into the ship, we saw several black merchants coming on board.

Source K

Olaudah Equiano was living in what is now Nigeria when he was captured at the age of 10 and taken to Virginia. He wrote about his experiences as a slave in a book published in 1789:

I was soon put down under the decks, and there I received such a greeting in my nostrils as I had never experienced in my life. I now wished for the last friend, death, to relieve me. The closeness of the place, and the heat of the climate, added to the number in the ship, which was so crowded that each had scarcely room to turn himself, almost suffocated us. The air soon became unfit for respiration, from a variety of loathsome smells, and brought on a sickness among the slaves, many of which died. The wretched situation was aggravated by the chains and the filth of the tubs, into which the children often fell, and were almost suffocated. The shrieks of the women, and the groans of the dying, rendered the whole a scene of horror.

Plantation slavery in North America

The first Africans arrived in North America during the early days of English colonisation, in 1619. Slavery developed quite slowly in North America, increasing as the growth of the tobacco trade during the 17th century created a demand for workers. By the middle of the 18th century there were over 260,000 African slaves in Virginia alone, most of whom had been transported to, rather than born in, the colony. A few years later the numbers decreased as the tobacco trade reduced, only to increase again with the introduction of cotton as a plantation crop, particularly after the invention of the cotton 'gin' in 1793 by Eli Whitney, an American from Connecticut.

The gin was an engine which speeded up the process of separating the fleecy white cotton fibre from the tough seeds. This made it possible to supply a rapidly expanding textile industry in Britain and, as a result, plantation owners required many more slaves to work in the cotton fields.

The slaves who survived the Atlantic crossing and reached North America were sold at slave auctions held regularly at large ports and towns, and subsequently put to work on the cotton, tobacco, sugar beet and rice plantations which developed in the southern states during the 17th and 18th centuries. The wealth of the plantation owners depended on plantation slavery which was known as 'The Peculiar Institution of the South' but was actually one of the most cruel of human systems. Between 1526 and 1870 about 10 million Africans were shipped to the Americas. Some people say this estimate is far too low. This figure does not allow for all those people who died in the process of enslavement and imprisonment in Africa while they awaited the European slave traders.

Numbers of Africans exported to the Americas

From 1526 to 1870 about 10 million slaves were shipped from Africa to:

Brazil	3,647,000
British Caribbean	1,665,000
French America	1,600,000
Spanish America	1,552,000
Dutch America	500,000
British North America and United States	399,000
Danish West Indies	28,000

1 Look at pages 8–9. Explain in your own words how the slave trade was organised.

2 Look at Sources E, J and K. What was it like to be transported as a slave from Africa to America?

3 a Skim through the whole of this unit. What information can you find to explain why slavery developed in the Americas?

b Explain in your own words how the cotton gin caused a need for more slaves.

To be sold as a slave

When they finally reached America Africans were sold, often in a brutal and terrifying manner.

What was it like to be sold as a slave?

The 'scramble'

Slaves brought to the Americas were distributed in different ways. One method, which must have been horrifying to the newly arrived slaves, was known as a 'scramble'. When the slave ships reached port their cargoes were herded together to be sold, either on deck or in a nearby yard. Sometimes they were sold at a fixed price per head, rather than being auctioned, and the purchasers would rush upon them, grabbing those they wanted to buy.

Sales and auctions

Many slaves were unloaded and held in slave pens to be sold at a later date. The most common form of slave sale was public auction – a method which was also used when slaves were re-sold.

Being sold by auction was a very cruel and frightening experience for a slave. In ports such as Charleston and Savannah they were often paraded in front of white buyers and examined like animals.

Slaves were made to stand on an auction block whilst the bidding took place. Often auctions took place 'by inch of candle', which meant bids were received until an inch of candle had burned. Families of slaves were sometimes kept together when sold, but usually children were taken from their parents and husbands and wives were separated.

A modern artist's impression of a 'scramble' based on the description by Alexander Falconbridge in Source A.

Source A

An English surgeon called Alexander Falconbridge described the following 'scramble' on land at Port Maria, Jamaica in the 1780s:

> On a day appointed the negroes were landed, and placed in a large yard belonging to the merchants to whom the ship is consigned. As soon as the hour agreed on arrived, the doors of the yard were suddenly thrown open, and in rushed a considerable number of purchasers, with all the ferocity of brutes. Some instantly seized such of the negroes as they could conveniently lay hold of with their hands. Others, being prepared with several handkerchiefs tied together, encircled with these as many as they were able. While others, by means of a rope, effected the same purpose. It is scarcely possible to describe the confusion.

Source B

Solomon Northup described his experience of being sold to a man in Louisiana in his autobiography:

> The men were arranged on one side of the room, the women at the other. We were paraded and made to dance. Bob, a coloured boy, who played the violin, would make us hold up our heads, walk briskly back and forth, while customers would feel our hands and arms and bodies, turn us about, ask us what we could do, make us open our mouths, and show our teeth, precisely as a jockey examines a horse which he is about to barter. Scars upon a slave's back were considered evidence of a rebellious spirit, and hurt his sale.

Twelve Years a Slave, 1853

Source C

In her autobiography called *Life of a Slave Girl*, Harriet Jacobs describes what happened to a slave in South Carolina when her children were sold:

> I saw a mother lead seven children to the auction block. She knew that some of them would be taken from her; but they took all. The children were sold to a slave-trader, and the mother was bought by a man in her own town. Before night her children were all far away. She begged the trader to tell her where he intended to take them; this he refused to do. How could he, when he knew he would sell them, one by one, wherever he could command the highest price? I met the mother in the street, and her wild, haggard face lives today in my mind. She wrung her hands in anguish, and exclaimed, 'Gone! All gone! Why don't God kill me? Slavery is terrible.'

Harriet Jacobs, 1861

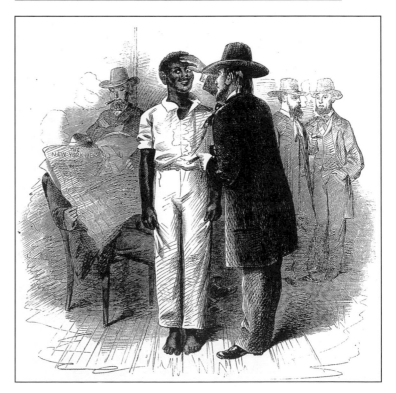

Source D

A wood engraving, based on a sketch made by Frank Vizetelly, called Dealers Inspecting a Negro at a Slave Auction in Virginia, *published in the* Illustrated London News, *18 July 1861.*

Branded and sold like cattle

Prices paid varied greatly depending on whether the slaves were young or old, well or ill. Slave owners would pay less for newly arrived slaves than for those who had been trained or who possessed valuable skills. Slaves who had already worked on the plantations and shown their abilities could be sold for a relatively high price. In the records of one plantation in Jamaica for the year 1787, there is an entry showing £330 being paid for a good mill carpenter named Jimmy, while on the same page is found Quamina 'a good watchman, but bad legs' valued at 6d (2.5p). On the other hand, unhealthy slaves who had just arrived but who could not be sold were regarded as valueless and were often left to die on the wharfs without food or water.

Upon purchase, slaves who had just arrived were given a European name in an attempt to make them forget their African past. They were usually branded like cattle with their owner's initials or mark on the face, chest or shoulder. In 1838, a slave owner in North Carolina, in the United States, advertised a slave as having been 'burnt with a hot iron on the left side of her face; I have tried to make the letter M.' In 1848, a Kentuckian described his runaway slave called Jane as having a brand mark 'on the breast something like L blotched.'

Source E

An example of a branding iron used to burn the owner's initials or mark into the flesh of a slave.

Source F

A description and engraving of a slave called Wilson Chinn, published in *Harper's Weekly* on 30 January 1864:

Wilson Chinn is about 60 years old, he was 'raised' by Isaac Howard of Woodford County, Kentucky. When 21 years old he was taken down the river and sold to Wolsey B. Marmillion, a sugar planter about 45 miles above New Orleans. This man was accustomed to brand his negroes, and Wilson has on his forehead the letters 'W.B.M.'. Slaves on this plantation were branded like cattle with a hot iron on the forehead, the breast or the arm.

14

Source G

The Slave Market *by Friedrich Schulz (1823–75). The auctioneer accepts a bid for a slave while prospective buyers inspect others awaiting sale.*

Source H

Englishman G. H. Andrews travelled with Frank Vizetelly, and sent this report on a slave auction in Richmond, Virginia, which was published in the *Illustrated London News* on 16 February 1861:

The auction-rooms for the sale of negroes are situated in the main streets, the only indications of the trade being a small red flag hanging from the front door-post, and a piece of paper upon which is written with pen and ink this simple announcement – 'Negroes for sale at auction this day at ten o'clock,' or whatever other time the sale is fixed for. At length a fine-looking coloured man was put forward. He walked straight up to the block, mounted it, and put himself in a most dignified attitude. The crier described the negro as of such an age, such a height, sound in wind and limb, as being a good farm hand, could guide a plough, shoe a horse, and mend a hoe, but was not a first rate smith. Then the biddings commenced, and 800 dollars were offered. This was the first human being I had ever seen being sold, and during the time of the biddings I felt the greatest difficulty in preventing myself from fainting. A dreadful sickness came over me, which defied all my efforts to conquer but being able to get some iced water, I got over this, my first visit to a slave auction.

Source I

A handbill advertising the 'Stafford Gang' of slaves for sale in 1855. The advertisement says that these slaves were 'acclimated'. This means that they were supposed to have been in America long enough to have become used to the conditions of their life of slavery.

John Judkyn Memorial

---

1 a What was a 'scramble'?
　b How were slave auctions organised?
2 What can we learn from the sources about how slaves were treated during sales? Do the sources all agree about conditions at a sale?
3 Imagine that you are a British journalist visiting the southern states in 1860. Using information from the unit, write an article describing how slaves were sold.

A life of slavery

Most slaves were bought by plantation owners who put the slaves to work growing sugar, cotton, tobacco and other crops. There were also large numbers of slaves in towns doing all sorts of manual work.

What sort of life did these slaves lead?

Working in the fields

Millions of black slaves were transported to the Americas to supply a mass labour force in order to grow crops on large plantations. Sugar-cane was largely grown in the West Indies. Cotton, tobacco and rice were cultivated in North America, and coffee and sugar in Central and South America.

In the West Indies the strongest men and women cleared the land, dug and planted the sugar-canes and, in crop time, cut the ripe canes or worked in the mill-house. Bigger boys and girls, as well as the old and infirm slaves, did most of the weeding and young children tended the garden and collected feed for the animals.

On plantations in North America, children began work at 5 or 6 years of age as 'water-toters'. When they were about 10 years old they began general work in the fields as 'quarter hands' and advanced to 'half hands', 'three-quarter hands' and when 18 years old became 'full hands'. As they grew old they started down this scale, ending life as a 'quarter hand' again. Very hard work, regular punishment, poor diet and lack of proper medical care meant that many slaves died young.

House servants

On the large plantations, slaves were divided into either house servants or field hands. House servants had many different jobs such as coachmen, cooks, butlers, housemaids, and children's nurses. They were often dressed in finer clothing and given a better diet than field hands.

The Granger Collection, New York

Source A
Slaves picking cotton on a plantation in Mississippi, USA.

Source B

According to this white author, slaves were often well treated:

> Mammy Harriet had fond memories of slavery days. 'Oh, no we was nebber hurried. Marster nebber once said, "Get up an' go to work," an' no oberseer ebber said it, either. Ef some on 'em did not git up when de odders went out to work, marster nebber said a word. Oh, no we was nebber hurried.'

Susan Smedes, *Memorials of a Southern Planter*, 1887

Source C

A former slave had a different view of treatment on a plantation in Louisiana:

> The hands are required to be in the cotton field as soon as it is light in the morning, and, with the exception of ten or fifteen minutes, which is given them at noon to swallow their allowance of cold bacon, they are not permitted to be a moment idle until it is too dark to see, and when the moon is full, they often labour till the middle of the night.

Solomon Northup, *Twelve Years a Slave*, 1853

Living conditions

Clothes were of the coarsest wool or cotton called 'homespun'. Children went shoeless even in winter. Food was monotonous: corn meal or sweet potato might be varied by food from the slaves' vegetable plots, if they were permitted. When meat was available it was of poor quality. Housing varied but usually consisted of one overcrowded room. The slave quarters were usually set in rows behind the big white house where the plantation owner lived. Overcrowded conditions with poor sanitation were a perfect breeding ground for disease.

Source D

William Russell, a reporter for *The Times* of London, visited the United States in 1861, and wrote the following description of slave quarters on Barnwell Island in South Carolina:

> The huts stand in a row, like a street, each with a poultry-house of rude planks behind it. No attempt at any drainage or any convenience existed near them. Heaps of oyster shells, broken crockery, old shoes, rags, and feathers were found near each hut. The huts were all alike window-less, and the apertures were generally filled up with a deal of board.

John Judkyn Memorial

Source E

A photograph of a family of slaves posing in front of their cabin on a plantation in one of the southern states.

Punishment

During the 1660s, laws called 'slave codes' were introduced in the British colonies in North America. These codes stated the meals that slaves were to receive, the clothing they were to be allowed, and the punishments to be given for certain offences, such as running away. Owners, however, were able to ignore these regulations without difficulty – slaves had no legal or civil rights – and very severe punishment was a regular part of plantation life.

Source F

A punishment ordered in Jamaica in 1767:

> Thunder, for running away – to have his right leg cut off below the knee, by a surgeon, at the owner's expense, within ten days.

R. Hart, *Slaves Who Abolished Slavery*, 1980

The whip was the most common tool of punishment. Punishment would be given out by the white overseer whose job on the plantation was to make sure the field hands worked hard all day long. Sometimes his orders were carried out by a black driver, often chosen from the ranks of the skilled slaves. Usually a flogging consisted of fifteen or twenty lashes on the back. The types of whips used varied from the 'rawhide', which cut into the skin after just a few strokes, to a leather strap which stung skin without cutting it. Some owners employed professional 'slave breakers' who brutally forced new or young slaves to submit to the system of extremely hard work.

Source G

Rules and Regulations for the Government of a Southern Plantation by a Mississippi Planter:

> Rule 8. Whipping, when necessary, shall be in moderation, and never done in a passion; and the driver shall in no instance inflict punishment, except in the presence of the overseer.

The complete set of these rules and regulations were published in a southern newspaper called the *Unionville Journal* on 16 July 1851

Source H

> Who could remain unmoved, to see a fellow-creature thus tied, unable to move or to raise a hand in his own defence; scourged on his bare back, with a cowhide, until the blood flows in streams from his quivering flesh? And for what? Often for the most trifling fault; and, as sometimes occurs, because a mere whim of his brutal overseer demands it.

Austin Steward, *Twenty-two Years a Slave, and Forty Years a Freeman*, 1857

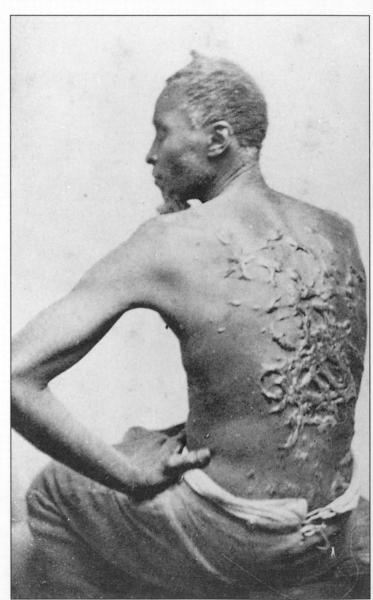

The Western Reserve Historical Society, Cleveland, Ohio

Source I
A photograph of an escaped slave called Gordon taken in 1863.

Source J

An instrument of torture among slaveholders

I send you the sketch of an instrument used by the slave-masters of Missouri to punish their negroes. Not long since, one of these wretched victims arrived here with an instrument of this description round his neck. It was securely riveted there, and required an hour's filing before it could be removed.

The instrument prevented him from lying down and taking his rest at night; and its weight and close fit rendered it very burdensome during the day. It consisted of a heavy iron ring, fitting closely round the neck, from which extended three prongs, each two feet in length, with a ring on the end. This negro had been running loose, with this thing round his neck, for two months.

Harper's Weekly, 15 February 1862

Fetters, or shackles, were usually used to control and punish runaways. A slaveholder in Mississippi had his runaway Maria 'ironed with a shackle on each leg connected with a chain'. When he caught another escaped slave called Albert he 'had an iron collar put on his neck'. Iron collars with bells attached were fitted around the necks of slaves on a plantation in Kentucky. Fetters and collars did not always prevent slaves from running away. A slave named Peter was reported in a Louisiana newspaper called *The Picayune* to have 'on each foot an iron ring, with a small chain attached to it' when he escaped in 1847. Some slaves were locked in plantation jails, whilst others were locked in medieval-style stocks, and fed on bread and water.

A modern illustration based on the original engraving.

1 Compare Sources B and C.
   a In what way do these sources give a different view of slave life on a plantation?
   b Why do they give a different view?
2 **a** The photograph in Source E was probably taken after the slaves were freed in the United States. Why do you think that photographs of black people as slaves on plantations are rare?
   b Do you think that historians can trust photographs of slave life on plantations?
3 Explain the difference between field hands and house servants.
4 How were slaves punished by their owners?
5 Using evidence from the sources in this and previous units, explain why many slaves died before they reached the age of 40.

What was life like for black people living in towns, or working in industry?

Not all slaves lived on plantations. Skilled slaves were often owned or hired by companies to work in places such as sawmills, gristmills, mines and fisheries. On river boats they were used as deck hands and firemen. Slaves were used to build roads, canals, bridges and railroads, and many lived and worked in towns. By 1860, probably half a million slaves or bondsmen lived in the southern cities and towns of the USA where they worked in virtually every skilled and unskilled occupation. Many of them were hired from plantation owners, and were made to wear numbered copper tags around their necks as a form of identification. Virtually all servants in large and many small town houses such as cooks, housekeepers and gardeners, were blacks. Other servants were employed in hotels. Town slaves also worked in cotton presses, tanneries, shipyards and bakehouses, and mastered the skills of the cabinet-maker and cobbler.

Source K

A visitor to Natchez, Mississippi, observed that town slaves included mechanics, draymen, hostlers, labourers, hucksters, and washwomen, and the multitude of every occupation, who filled the streets of a busy city – for slaves are trained to every kind of manual labour. The blacksmith, cabinet-maker, carpenter, builder, wheelwright, all have one or more slaves labouring at their trades. The negro is a third arm to every working man, who can possibly save enough to purchase one.

Joseph H. Ingraham, *The South-West, by a Yankee*, 1835

Source L

The Dandy Slave: a Scene in Baltimore, Maryland, 1861

The Granger Collection, New York

A sketch by Frank Vizetelly, and accompanying caption by G. H. Andrews, published in the Illustrated London News *on 6 August 1861.*

One rainy Sunday, in Baltimore, our Artist saw and sketched one of these dandy negroes escorting home from church his mistress. He was a slave, and this poor old faded woman owned him. He was proud and fond of her, and she, no doubt, not a little attached to him. 'Oh,' he said, 'my misses is a very good misses; fine old lady; lets me do pretty much as I'm a mind 'ter. If I feels like work, I works. I ollers gives her half my wages, and she never asks no questions. Oh, lor, no; I wouldn't think of running away, or doing nothing that could noways annoy her. I gets plenty of money; hire myself down on steam-boat, sir. I'm very good waiter; the ladies mostly likes me; and steam-boat captain likes to have waiters as is pop'lar with the ladies. I never gives no sass to nobody. It's very easy getting along when you make it a rule never to give no sass to nobody.'

Free blacks

Occasionally, town slaves managed to buy their own freedom. Often, they were allowed to hire themselves to others for a fee. Half of the money had to be given to their owners, but the other half could be saved towards the price of their freedom – a sum which was decided by their owners. This purchase of liberty was called 'manumission'. By 1860 there were about 265,600 free blacks in the southern states.

Source O

Numbered copper tags like this were tied around the necks of slaves who worked and lived in towns and cities in the United States.   John Judkyn Memorial

---

Source M

A list of the number of black people arrested and locked in the Guard House at Columbia, South Carolina, during December 1861:

Slaves

By order of owner	20
Out after hours	34
Disorderly conduct	8
Drunk	3
Runaway	2
In the city without ticket	1
Stealing	3
Drunk and disorderly	1
	72

Free blacks

Drunk and disorderly	1
Stealing	2
	3

Source N

The slaves are much addicted to theft but the free blacks much more so. They, poor wretches, have the bad privilege of getting drunk, and they avail themselves of it. The heaviest scourge of New Orleans is its multitudes of free black and coloured people. They wallow in debauchery, are quarrelsome and saucy, and commit crimes, in proportion to slaves as a hundred to one.

Timothy Flint, *Recollections of the Last Ten Years in the Valley of the Mississippi*, 1826

---

1 Study Source K. What can we learn from this source about the work of slaves in towns?

2 Study Source L.

   a Describe in your own words the lifestyle of this slave.

   b In what way is this source useful for showing the difference in the lives of town and plantation slaves?

   c Do you think the slave in this source had a typical owner? Give reasons for your answer.

3 Study Source O. Why were slaves in towns and industry made to wear a numbered copper tag tied around their necks?

4 Look at Sources M and N. How useful are they for a historian investigating the life of slaves in town? How far can these sources be trusted?

5 'Blacks played an important role in town life and industry in the southern states between the years 1800 and 1861.' Use all the sources in this unit to discuss whether you agree or disagree with this statement.

The fight for freedom, 1699-1865

In 1791 a revolt began among the 'maroons', or escaped slaves, on the island of St Domingue in the West Indies. Led by Toussaint L'Ouverture, who had once been a slave, they defeated first the French and then the British and gained independence in 1800. They renamed the island Haiti, which became the first black republic in the Americas.

Slaves revolted against their owners by running away. An escape route called the 'Underground Railroad' was set up in the United States during the 19th century, along which thousands of black people found safety and freedom in the northern states and in Canada.

Since 1787, William Wilberforce and Thomas Clarkson of the Abolition Society had worked to free the slaves in the British colonies. The British slave trade was ended in 1807, and slaves in the West Indies were told in 1834 that they would be free after working for another six years.

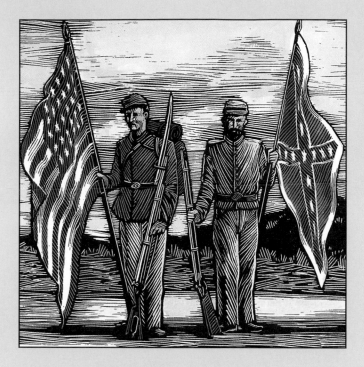

Between 1860 and 1861 the eleven slave states in the USA left the Union, and the American Civil War began. The North, led by President Abraham Lincoln, invaded the South to force them back into the Union. Black people were used by both armies.

Between 1862 and 1863, black abolitionist Frederick Douglass helped to persuade President Lincoln to emancipate, or free, the slaves, and allow black soldiers to join the Union army. He travelled through the North raising black recruits who joined the 54th and 55th Massachusetts Volunteers at New Bedford.

On 18 July 1863 the 54th Massachusetts, commanded by Colonel Robert Gould Shaw, made their brave charge on Fort Wagner in Charleston Harbor. Following this, President Lincoln decided to allow more black soldiers to take part in battles. By 1865, a total of 178,892 black soldiers had helped to end slavery and win the war.

4

Revolt and resistance

Throughout the centuries of slavery there were many examples
of revolt and resistance. Most were unsuccessful but some
slaves regained their liberty.

How did black people try to win back their freedom?

Throughout the history of their enslavement there is
evidence of Africans resisting and fighting back.
Sometimes they managed to revolt on board the ship
which was carrying them to the Americas. At least 59
such revolts occurred between 1699 and 1845. One of the
most successful took place in 1839 when Joseph Cinque,
son of an African king, led 54 slaves in revolt aboard the
Spanish ship *Amistad*. He and his men seized the ship and
tried to sail back to Africa but the crew of the ship tricked
Cinque and he mistakenly landed on the Long Island
coast of New York in the United States and was
recaptured. Cinque and others were finally freed by the
Supreme Court of the United States after a lengthy legal
case brought by local abolitionists.

Revolution in the Caribbean

Encouraged by the French Revolution, with its slogan
'Liberty, Equality, Fraternity', unsuccessful slave revolts
took place in the French territories of Martinique and
Guadeloupe in the Caribbean in 1789. In 1791, the
maroons, led by Toussaint L'Ouverture, successfully
revolted on the partly French-held island of St
Domingue – the greatest wealth-producing colony in the
New World. By 1800 St Domingue was free from colonial
rule, and was renamed Haiti, with L'Ouverture as its
ruler. Although the army of Napoleon Bonaparte
attempted to reconquer Haiti in 1801, and managed to
trick L'Ouverture into captivity, another maroon leader
called Jean-Jacques Dessalines defeated the French and
on 1 January 1804 declared Haiti totally independent.

Source A

*Toussaint
L'Ouverture.*

The Granger Collection,
New York

Source B

In overthrowing me, they have felled in Saint
Domingue only the trunk of the tree of Negro liberty;
it will shoot forth from the roots, because they are
deep and numerous.

Toussaint L'Ouverture, 1802

Resistance in the United States

The bloodiest slave revolt in the USA occurred on 21 August 1831 when Nat Turner and six other slaves in Southampton County, Virginia, attacked their master and family as they lay sleeping in their beds at night. Turner had earlier seen visions and heard voices which convinced him that it was right to rebel against white rule. During the next few days 55 whites were murdered with swords and hatchets as other slaves joined the rebellion. Pursued by the army and local militia, Turner's followers eventually dwindled away during the next 10 weeks, until he was captured in a hideout dug in the ground beneath a fallen tree in the Great Dismal Swamp. Tried and found guilty of insurrection and plotting to kill 'free white persons', Turner and 16 of his followers were hanged on 11 November 1831.

Source D

The rebellion terrified the state. Properties were temporarily abandoned in the county and rumours of uprisings in neighbouring areas were rife. Overnight the abolition [freedom] movement lost most of its support in the South, and slave codes were tightened in many states. In Virginia, for example, slaves were barred from attending religious teachings or meetings conducted by whites without their master's consent, and it was made illegal to write or print anything likely to cause slave revolt.

Henry Steele Commager, *The American Destiny*, 1986

Source C

A contemporary coloured engraving of the capture of Nat Turner.

The Granger Collection, New York

The 'John Brown' rebellion

On 16 October, 1859, a white abolitionist called John Brown attempted to start a slave rebellion by seizing the government arsenal at Harper's Ferry in Virginia. He planned to take the captured weapons to the local town slaves whom he hoped would join his 'freedom army'. With just 21 followers, including four of his sons, four free blacks and one escaped slave he successfully seized the arsenal. He took several hostages, one of whom was Colonel Lewis Washington, a local slave owner, and great-grand nephew of the first president. Then his plans failed. Militia and angry townsfolk quickly surrounded the engine house at Harper's Ferry where Brown and his men were trapped, and began shooting at its occupants. The slaves were not supplied with weapons as planned. Brown's men fought on but the first person they killed was the railroad baggage master – a free black. The engine house was finally stormed by 90 US Marines led by Lieutenant-Colonel Robert E. Lee, who eventually became the Commander of the Southern, or Confederate, Army during the American Civil War. Brown was wounded and captured, and nine of his followers were killed, including two of his sons. One black managed to escape, and was never captured. The remaining rebels, including John Brown, were publicly hanged at Charlestown, Virginia later that year. Although many Northerners disapproved of John Brown's methods, his attempted rebellion at Harper's Ferry persuaded many of them that slavery in the United States had to be abolished, and convinced many Southerners that slavery had to be defended.

Source F

US Marines storm the engine house at Harper's Ferry.

Source E

I believe that to have interfered as I have done in behalf of His despised poor, is no wrong, but right. Now, if it is deemed necessary that I should forfeit my life for the furtherance of the ends of justice, and mingle my blood further with the blood of millions in this slave country whose rights are disregarded by wicked, cruel, and unjust enactments, I say, let it be done.

John Brown at the end of his trial in 1859

Day-to-day resistance

The great majority of slaves did not take part in spectacular revolts. Nevertheless they were able to show their defiance and contempt for slave-owning whites in many aspects of their daily lives. They kept part of their rich African culture alive through song and dance. Many songs celebrated the dream of freedom. Music was a powerful way of expressing solidarity and identity.

The former slave and black leader, Frederick Douglass, described how he and other slaves felt justified in stealing from white people. For Douglass, white people lost all rights when they treated him as a piece of property rather than as a human being. He said: 'Since [white] society has marked me out as plunder, I am justified in plundering in return.'

Whites often commented on the solidarity of slaves and the fact that it was very unusual for one slave to betray another. A strong sense of community helped slaves deal with the appalling treatment they received from their owners. Within the community the greatest respect was given to those who successfully defied the whites.

A modern artist's impression of John Brown and his followers inside the engine house at Harper's Ferry just before the US Marines broke in.

Source G

A modern black American summarises the values of the slave community in the 19th century:

Survival was good. Outwitting the master was good. Helping others to survive was good. Stealing from black people was bad.

The community had special heroes. The bold rebel who challenged the system and survived was admired by almost everyone. The slave the overseer was afraid to whip, the slave who ran away and made it to the North, the woman who talked back and got away with it: these were the ideal types.

Lerone Bennett, *The Shaping of Black America*, 1991

1 Show on a timeline each of the revolts against slavery described in this unit. For each revolt explain whether or not it was successful.
2 How many different motives for rebellion can you find in these examples?
3 Imagine that you are a radio producer. You want to produce a programme on one important example of how people fought against slavery. Which example will you choose? Explain your choice.

Runaways

From the earliest days of slavery, there were slaves who ran away to try to find freedom. In the first half of the 19th century many slaves fled to Canada.

What happened to these runaways?

'Cimarrones'

In the Spanish colonies of the Americas, runaway slaves called 'cimarrones' or 'maroons', escaped into the jungles and forests where they lived in hidden settlements. Although the number of runaways was never very great in the United States, a steady stream of advertisements for fugitives in southern newspapers shows that throughout the period of slavery there were always those who were prepared to take great risks in order to achieve their freedom.

Who were these runaways? They were generally young slaves, most of them under thirty. The majority of them were males, though female runaways were not unknown. Some slaves tried running away only once and were caught, whilst others made repeated attempts until they were finally free. Runaways usually went singly or in small groups of two or three. But some escaped in groups of a dozen or more, and in a few instances in groups of more than 50.

Slaves were required to carry passes from their masters, and free blacks had to have papers which described them clearly and stated that they were not slaves. The use of stolen, borrowed or forged passes or free papers was common with runaways. Some bold fugitives tried to work and live as free men and women in the South.

The 'Underground Railroad'

In the early 19th century most runaway slaves tried to escape to the northern states and to Canada along the 'Underground Railroad', the name given to those people prepared to help them to safety. Travelling mostly at night, and using the North Star as their guide, it was estimated in 1855 that 'upwards of 60,000 slaves' had been assisted to freedom. The hiding places along the route were called stations and those who helped transport the slaves were known as conductors.

A modern illustration showing exhausted runaways as they reach a farm in Newport, Indiana, a way station on the Underground Railroad to Canada.

The Fugitive Slave Laws

A Fugitive Slave Law, passed in 1793, made it illegal to hide runaways. In 1850 government officers and police were given the power to recapture runaways. Anyone who helped a slave escape could be fined $2,000 and given six months in jail. Professional slave catchers scoured northern cities looking for fugitives. Many of the 200,000 free blacks living in the North, frightened of being kidnapped, fled to Canada.

Source A

A poster produced in 1851 warning blacks in the North against slave catchers.

The Granger Collection, New York

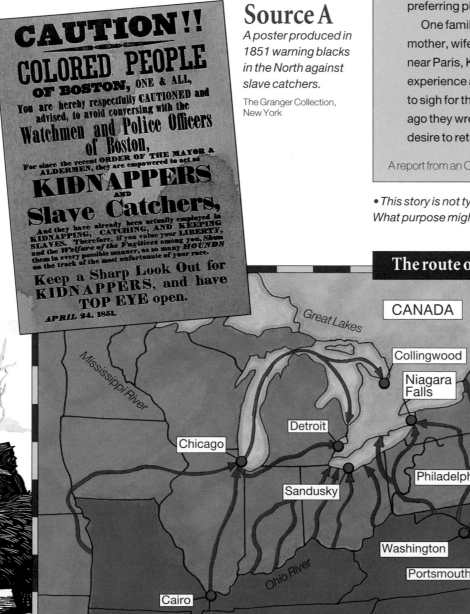

Source B

The packet *Union* arrived from Port Stanley, Canada, with sixteen fugitive slaves, who had escaped from the South within the last two years, and had been living at the negro settlement at Chatham, West Canada. Becoming weary of Canadian freedom which to many blacks embraces [holds] the liberty of going inadequately clothed, and of being nearly starved to death, they were about to return to the South, preferring plantation life.

One family, consisting of a coloured man, his mother, wife and three children, who escaped from near Paris, Kentucky, about one year ago, after the experience afforded by a hard Canadian winter, began to sigh for their 'Old Kentucky Home', and a short time ago they wrote to their master informing him of their desire to return.

A report from an Ohio newspaper, the *Cleveland Democrat*, 1859

• *This story is not typical of what successful runaways chose to do. What purpose might the writer have in publishing such a story?*

The route of the Underground Railroad

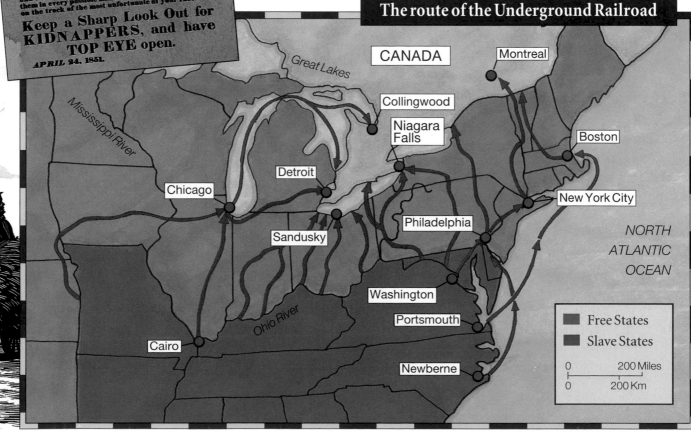

Free States
Slave States

0   200 Miles
0   200 Km

NORTH ATLANTIC OCEAN

John Anderson

Born a slave about 1830, John Anderson was originally owned by Moses Burton, a tobacco farmer in Fayette, Howard County, Mississippi. His mother was sold and parted from him when he was seven years old. He was sold for $1,000 when he reached manhood. He married at Christmas 1850 and began to raise a family in slavery, but in 1853 he was parted from his wife and baby when he was again sold to a plantation about 30 miles away. Forbidden to visit his family, John escaped about six weeks later. After just three days on the run, he stabbed to death a slave catcher called Seneca Diggs, who tried to recapture him. He fled to Canada where he settled but he was arrested in 1860, and put on trial for the murder of Seneca Diggs. His trial was reported in Canadian, American and European newspapers, and drew sympathy from many people in England because the Canadian judges ruled that John should be sent back to the United States, and returned to slavery. The British government wrote to the Governor-General of Canada asking that Anderson should not be surrendered. Anderson was invited to Britain and was in London by the beginning of August 1861, where he attended the 27th anniversary celebrations of the emancipation, or setting free, of the slaves in the West Indies. After a year of education at Northamptonshire, Anderson went to Liberia, the independent African state established by Americans in 1822.

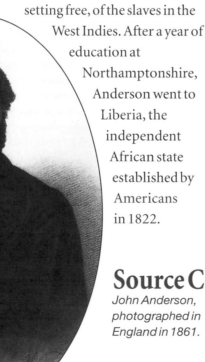

Source C

John Anderson, photographed in England in 1861.

The Granger Collection, New York

Source D

Advertisements, like this one printed in Kentucky in 1838, usually gave detailed descriptions of runaway slaves.

Source E

John Anderson explains why he killed Seneca Diggs:

He [Seneca Diggs] said, 'Where are you going?' I said I was making my way to some farmer's house. He said, 'I will go with you, you are a runaway.' I tried to escape, and he chased me for half a day. He came to take me, and I struck him a blow. He came again, and I struck him again on the left side, and he came no more.

---

1 How did slave owners try to get back any runaway slaves?

2 Explain in your own words how the 'Underground Railroad' worked.

3 Imagine that you are in London in 1862. You meet the famous former slave John Anderson just before his departure for Liberia. Write the script of a conversation with Anderson in which he explains his remarkable life story.

Abolitionists

In the late 18th and 19th centuries many people in America and Europe began to call for an end to slavery. They were called abolitionists.

Who were the abolitionists and what did they do?

Abolitionists and the British Empire

The trade in African slaves was ended before slavery itself. An Abolition Society was founded in Britain in 1787. Its leading figure was Thomas Clarkson, who travelled through Britain speaking out against the slave trade, and persuading people not to buy slave-grown sugar. In Parliament an MP called William Wilberforce demanded abolition. The British government finally abolished the slave trade in 1807, which meant that no more slaves would be carried from Africa in British ships.

Other nations, such as the United States of America, followed the British example and also abolished the slave trade soon after.

Although the British Parliament ended the slave trade in 1807, slavery in the British West Indies continued until 1834. In that year a law was passed called the Emancipation Act. According to this law, slaves under six years of age in British colonies such as Jamaica and Barbados became absolutely free. Field hands over six years old had to carry on working for their owners for six years; house slaves had to work for another ten years. Meanwhile the British government gave former slave owners £20 million in compensation, whilst the slaves got nothing. The new system did not work well, and in 1838 all ex-slaves were given complete freedom. Although they were no longer slaves, black people in the British West Indies remained poor and the whites remained powerful and wealthy.

Source A
Thomas Clarkson.

Abolitionists in the USA

There were a few white abolitionists from the earliest days of American independence. Local abolitionist groups were set up, the first of which was the Pennsylvania Society for Promoting the Abolition of Slavery, founded in 1775. Abolitionist groups were stronger in the North than in the South. From the mid-1770s, individual northern states began to abolish slavery until, in 1827, slavery was banned throughout the North.

The first white-controlled abolitionist groups were not at all militant. They wanted slave owners to be given compensation. From the 1820s more free black people became involved and abolitionists began to take a tougher attitude towards slave owners. In 1829 a man called David Walker published a pamphlet calling on black slaves to use force if necessary to get freedom.

The abolition movement grew in strength in the 1830s and 1840s. In 1833 the American Anti-Slavery Society was established. Within five years its membership had grown to 250,000. This organisation had both white and black members. William Garrison, a white man, set up an abolitionist newspaper called the *Liberator* in 1833.

Many ex-slaves became active abolitionists. Some wrote memoirs of their lives in slavery as part of the campaign. One of the most outstanding black abolitionists was Frederick Douglass. He was born a slave in Maryland in 1817 but escaped in 1838. He wrote a powerful best-selling book about his time as a slave. A brilliant public speaker, Douglass travelled all over the world raising support for the anti-slavery movement.

Source B

Remember, Americans, that we must and shall be free and enlightened as you are, will you wait until we shall, under God, obtain our liberty by the crushing arm of power? I declare to you, while you keep us and our children in bondage, and treat us like brutes, to make us support you and your families, we cannot be your friends. Treat us like men, and we will be your friends.

Extract from a pamphlet written by David Walker in 1829

Source D

Frederick Douglass.

The Granger Collection, New York

Source C

A banner used by the American abolitionists.

THIS IS THE LORD'S DOING.

SLAVERY ABOLISHED IN THE BRITISH WEST-INDIES AUGUST 1ST 1854.

LAUS DEO.

Source E

Douglass argued that black people should take the lead in abolitionist organisations:

It is our battle, no one else can fight for us, our relations to the anti-slavery movement must be changed. Instead of depending upon it, we must lead it.

Frederick Douglass, 1854

32

Women ex-slaves played a major role in the abolitionist struggle. Harriet Tubman was born a slave in Maryland in 1823. After 25 years of slavery, she successfully escaped from her master, but returned south many times to rescue other slaves. She founded the Fugitives' Aid Society, which gave help to blacks who settled in Canada.

Another prominent black woman was Sojourner Truth. After escaping from slavery in 1827 she became a leading public speaker for the abolitionist movement. She also campaigned for equal rights for women.

Source F

Harriet Tubman. This photograph was taken in about 1860. It was coloured by painting oils over the photograph.

Source G

A painting of Sojourner Truth painted in 1864.

Source H

A description of a meeting with Harriet Tubman:

In Beaufort we spent nearly all our time at Harriet Tubman's – otherwise known as 'Moses'. She is a wonderful woman – a real heroine. Has helped off a large number of slaves, after taking her own freedom. She told us that she used to hide them in the woods during the day. Once she had with her a man named Joe, for whom a reward of $1500 was offered. At last they reached safety in Suspension Bridge over the Falls and found themselves in Canada. Until then, she said, Joe had been very silent. But when she said 'Now we are in Canada', he sprang to his feet with a great shout, and sang and clapped his hands in a perfect delirium of joy. How exciting it was to hear her tell the story. My own eyes were full as I listened to her. I am glad I saw her – very glad.

Charlotte Forten, 1863

Although black people played a very active part in the abolitionist movement after 1830, white supporters also remained active. In 1852 a white writer called Harriet Beecher Stowe published a novel entitled *Uncle Tom's Cabin*. This told the story of an old slave who died after being beaten by an overseer. Selling 300,000 copies in just one year, this book did much to raise support for the abolitionist cause.

1 Explain in your own words how slavery was abolished in the British Empire.

2 Look at Sources B and E. What can we learn from these sources about the attitudes of black abolitionists towards white people?

3 What part did leading black women play in the abolitionist movement?

4 Using all the information in this unit, identify four different ways in which the abolition movement worked to free the slaves.

7

Contraband

During the American Civil War, black people were used by both sides. Large numbers of runaway slaves fled to the North. They were known as 'contrabands'.

What did the contrabands and other black people do during the American Civil War?

During the years 1830 to 1860, conflict grew between the North and South over the issue of slavery. The abolition movement in the North was hated by most southern slave owners, who feared the loss of their slave labour force. The northern states were going through an industrial revolution and needed more people to work in their factories. Some northern factory owners believed that, if freed, the slaves would leave the South and provide the workers they needed. In addition, the North wanted tariffs, or taxes, placed on imported foreign goods to protect their new industries. The mainly agricultural South depended on trade, and was therefore against import tariffs. When Abraham Lincoln was elected as President of the United States in 1860, eleven southern states, consisting of South Carolina, Mississippi, Florida, Alabama, Georgia, Louisiana, Texas, Virginia, Arkansas, North Carolina and Tennessee, decided to 'secede', or leave the Union, to form their own separate nation called the Confederate States of America. This resulted in the outbreak of a civil war, as the North invaded the South to force them back into the Union, whilst the South, or Confederacy, defended their newly declared independence.

The Confederate and United States of America

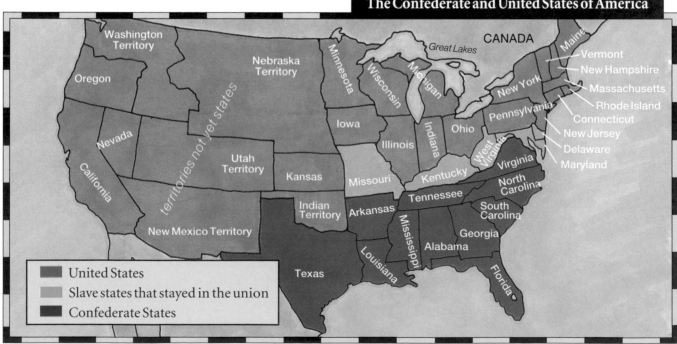

United States
Slave states that stayed in the union
Confederate States

Black people as 'Contraband of War'

In 1861 the slaves in Virginia, learning of the northern invasion, began to arrive at the camps of the Union soldiers in large numbers hoping to find freedom. At first, northern officers were unsure what to do about such great numbers of fugitives from the southern plantations, but Major-General Benjamin F. Butler, Union commander of Fort Monroe on the Jamestown Peninsula, promptly declared them to be 'contraband of war', because they were the property of the enemy. The word 'contraband' means illegal or smuggled goods. Henceforth, the term 'contraband' was used in the North to describe slaves who sought freedom among the northern troops. As the Union armies invaded the southern states thousands of 'contrabands' flocked into their camps and forts.

Source A

I was brought out with others to work cutting wood at the hospitals and I broke and run. They shot at me once. I got into a cellar and hid under some rags till dark. Then I slipped out of town and stayed with some friends. They took me through the woods and fields going that night about 12 miles. Came into Union pickets [sentries]. Got a pass from General Crittenden's aide to come into town to tell what I knew.

Statement of Charlie, a 'contraband', who escaped into Union lines in Tennessee on 23 December 1862

Source B

A gentleman recently from Washington, D.C., informs the *Richmond Examiner* that the stolen and runaway negroes from Virginia, to the number of three thousand and upwards, are encamped on the 'Slashes', within the northern precincts of the city. They are badly clothed, worse fed, and their scanty tents furnish but a poor shelter from the warring elements at this inclement season. Many have died, and numbers are dying every day from pneumonia and typhoid disease induced by their exposed condition.

A newspaper report from the Charleston Mercury, *12 January 1863*

A modern illustration of 'contrabands' arriving at Fort Monroe in Virginia.

Source C

'Contrabands' pause to have their photograph taken whilst unloading war supplies for the Union Army at Alexandria, Virginia.

Black people working for the Union

At the beginning of the war, 'contrabands' were not used to fight against the South. Their contribution as soldiers, later in the war, is described in the next chapter. Black people, however, were quickly employed as workers digging trenches and building forts for the Union soldiers. They were also set to work on captured plantations to pick and process cotton in order to help with the northern war effort. Others were employed on plantations in the Sea Islands on the coast of South Carolina, and were either offered part of the crop they grew, or given a wage ranging from $3 to $25 a month. Many more 'contrabands' were sent to the North to work in mills and factories, and on farms, and received a mixed reception. In order to increase their profits, employers hired them as cheap labour in place of white workers, who were often fired.

Source D

Headquarters of Vincent Collyer, the Superintendent of the Poor at Newberne, North Carolina, where captured

Source E

A journal in Madison county, Ohio, relates that a farmer turned off all his white farm hands, and employed eighteen negroes in their place, who were sent to that county by Colonel Moody, of the army. *The Patriot* [a newspaper], of Lancaster, in the same State, says: 'We hear of numerous cases in our immediate neighbourhood where white men have been turned away by their employers, to make room for 'contrabands,' whose services are obtained at half price.'

A report from a southern newspaper, the *Edgefield Advertiser*, dated 16 July 1862

Blacks in the Confederacy

As we have already seen, not all black people in the United States were slaves. In 1860 there was a significant minority of free blacks in the slave states. Though most were not much better off than slaves, some had jobs and trades. A few supported the Confederate States, and even offered money to equip the soldiers. Others volunteered unsuccessfully to fight in the southern army.

Source F

One hundred and twenty free negroes, uniformed with red shirts and dark pants, and bearing a flag of the southern Confederacy marched through the city of Petersburg, Virginia and embarked for Norfolk. They proceeded of their own free will to work upon the fortifications around Norfolk harbor.

This report was printed in a Confederate newspaper called the *Daily Richmond Enquirer*, 26 April 1861

• *The number of people involved in this work was a very small proportion of the free blacks in the Confederacy. Why do you think the newspaper printed this story?*

Source G

Some black servants and slaves were required to accompany their masters to battle.

George [a black slave] had just arrived in this city, from Virginia, in company with his young master, Capt. Robt. Hardy, having been with him since his departure from Georgia to the seat of war, and taken an active part in assisting his master's company at the battle of Manassas. George claims the glory of having shot one Yankee and taken another prisoner. In going for some water, George came across a stranger hid in a thicket, and from his dress suspected him an enemy. He walked up to him, with gun in hand, when the Yankee sung out that his gun was not loaded. George then took his gun and some papers and marched his prisoner to the Quartermaster's. The latter told George to retain the rifle as a keepsake.

A Confederate newspaper report, printed in the *Charleston Daily Courier*, 31 July 1861

• *How useful is this information as historical evidence of the attitudes of black people in the southern states?*

A modern illustration of blacks building fortifications for the Confederate Army at Savannah, Georgia.

Slaves used by the Confederate Army

Meanwhile, many other slaves were used unofficially in 1861 by the Confederate Army as labourers to dig trenches and to build fortifications. Many slave owners objected to this and tried to get their slaves back. With a growing shortage of soldiers, the use of blacks as a fighting force was seriously considered by some Confederate generals but the idea was rejected in case it caused a slave revolt. On 17 February 1864, the government passed a law ordering all free blacks between the ages of 18 and 50 to work in weapons factories, military hospitals, or building forts.

Slaves as Confederate soldiers

Finally, with the South close to defeat in 1865, General Robert E. Lee, the commander of the Confederate Army, asked that blacks be armed to defend the Confederacy. On 13 March 1865, a desperate Confederate government tried to enlist 300,000 blacks to be formed into special regiments. A few blacks may have actually seen combat in the Confederate Army.

Source H

We reproduce one of Mr. Mead's sketches. It illustrates the way in which the cowardly rebels force their negro slaves to do dangerous work. It represents a struggle between two negroes and a rebel captain, who insisted upon their loading a cannon within range of Berdan's Sharp-shooters [a northern regiment]. The affair was witnessed by our officers through a glass themselves, and they were shot, one after the other.

Harper's Weekly, 10 May 1862

Source I

Several thousand persons assembled in the Capitol Square [in Richmond, Virginia] this afternoon, to witness the parade of a battalion of troops including two companies of negroes. The battalion produced quite a sensation, chiefly among the negro population. The interest of the occasion was lessened by a failure to uniform and equip the negro soldiers. They were armed with muskets, and went through the manual as well as could be expected, for the short time they had been drilled. Several regiments of negroes are in the course of formation in different parts of Virginia.

A report printed in the *Edgefield Advertiser* of South Carolina, 29 March 1865

Source J

This is an extract from a letter written by a Union soldier on 9 March 1865 on the outskirts of Richmond, Virginia:

The First Corps advanced their picket line a short distance this morning, and it is reported to have found colored troops on picket line on their front. If this is true it shows that the rebels have at last adopted the policy of arming slaves.

Source K

A cartoon and caption published in the North by *Harper's Weekly* on 5 November 1864:

The time has come for us to put into the army every able-bodied negro man as a soldier. We have learned from dear-bought experience that negroes can be taught to fight. I would free all able to bear arms, and put them into the field at once. They will make much better soldiers with us than against us, and swell the now depleted ranks of our armies.

Henry W. Allen (Confederate Governor of Louisiana) to James W. Seddon (Confederate Secretary of War), 26 September 1864

---

1 a Explain the meaning of the term 'contrabands'.

b According to Source A, why were 'contrabands' valuable to the Union Army?

2 Study Sources B and E, both of which are southern newspaper reports of treatment experienced by 'contrabands' in the North.

a Is there any similarity in the content of these two reports?

b Why do you think newspapers in the South were keen to report stories like these?

3 Look at Sources C and D. What evidence is there in these pictures that 'contrabands' were being treated kindly by some northerners?

4 Using as much information as possible, explain how 'contrabands' were used by the North to help win the Civil War up to 1863.

5 a In what way did the Confederacy use blacks in the Civil War before 1865?

b Why do you think some slave owners objected to their slaves helping with the war effort by digging trenches and building forts?

6 Study Sources F and G. Explain in your own words what these sources tell us about some black people in the Confederacy.

7 a Explain what is going on in Source H.

b Study the caption for Source H and explain reasons why this source may not be totally reliable.

8 Study Source K. According to this cartoon, what did some white people in the northern states think would happen if the South included blacks in their armies?

9 Many films depict the American Civil War as a conflict between the whites of the Union and the whites of the Confederacy. Do you think this is an accurate view of the war?

8

'One gallant rush'

Black people made a vital contribution to the Union war effort.
Many black troops served in the Union Army.

What was the experience of black soldiers in the Union Army?

Black people in defence of the Union

Blacks were employed in the Union Army as servants and
labourers from the first days of the Civil War. The first
attempt to recruit them into the Union Army as soldiers
was made by Major-General David Hunter at Port Royal,
South Carolina, in April 1862. Known variously at first as
the 'First South Carolina Contraband Brigade' and the
'National Negro Brigade', it was poorly clothed and badly
paid. It did not officially become part of the Union Army
until it was re-named the 1st South Carolina Volunteer
Regiment. After this it was properly clothed, and led by
Colonel Thomas W. Higginson, of Massachusetts, until
he was seriously wounded in 1864.

Source A

Dear Sir

I have the honour to report that the organisation of
the 1st Regt. of South Carolina Volunteers is now
completed. I have never seen in any body of men
such enthusiasm and deep seated devotion to their
officers as exists in this. They will surely go wherever
they are led.

A letter from the Superintendent of Contrabands in South
Carolina to the Secretary of War, 25 January 1863

Source B

*'Before and after'
photographs of a
young man called
Jackson who was a
servant attached to
the Confederate
Army until he
escaped to the
Union Army,
becoming a
drummer boy in the
79th United States
Colored Troops.*

The large-scale recruitment of black troops did not begin until late 1862, and was mainly the work of ex-slave Frederick Douglass (see page 32), a self-educated lawyer from Virginia called John M. Langston, and Martin Delany, a doctor who had studied at Harvard and who later became an officer in the United States Army. Once in the army, blacks often faced unfair treatment, or discrimination, of every kind. Gradually, they were accepted as soldiers – although rarely as equals. Their pay varied from $7 to $10 a month, compared with the white soldiers' $13, until the closing months of the war, when they received equal pay. What changed the attitude of white soldiers more than anything else was the bravery of black soldiers in battle. During the last three years of the Civil War, black regiments in the Union Army took part in more than 33 major battles. Of the 178,892 blacks who fought for the Union, 32,369, or more than a sixth of their number, died in uniform. The northern government awarded at least 20 black soldiers with its newly created Medal of Honor.

Source D

The iron gate of our prison stands half open, one gallant rush will fling it wide.

A rallying cry used by Frederick Douglass during his recruiting campaign of 1862

Source E

Sir,
We The Members of Company D of the 55th Massachusetts Volunteers call the attention of your Excellency to our case. We have been in the field now thirteen months and a great many yet longer. We have received no pay and have been offered only seven dollars per month which the Paymaster has said was all he had ever been authorized to pay colored troops.

Extract from a letter sent to President Lincoln, 16 July 1864

Source C

Detail from a flag carried by the 3rd US Colored Troops.

RATHER DIE FREEMAN THAN LIVE TO BE SLAVES

3 UNITED STATES COLORED TROOPS

The 54th Massachusetts

The 54th and 55th Massachusetts Volunteers were the first two regiments of black troops officially ordered to be raised by the United States Government during the Civil War. Equipped and trained at New Bedford, Massachusetts, the 54th was commanded by Colonel Robert Gould Shaw, the son of a Boston abolitionist, and included two sons of Frederick Douglass in its ranks. Eventually sent into action on the South Carolina coast, this regiment sought to prove that black troops could fight as well as white soldiers. On 18 July 1863, 600 men of the 54th Massachusetts were ordered to lead an advance across a stretch of sandy beach to attack the Confederate strong point at Fort Wagner. With the capture of this fort, the port of Charleston, South Carolina, could be taken by northern forces. If the 54th Massachusetts had faltered in the face of the enemy cannon staring at them across the open beach, the North may have refused to put further black troops into battle. However, the brave attack of the 54th, supported by other troops, reached the walls of the fort under heavy gunfire.

Source F
Colonel Robert Gould Shaw

If the raising of colored troops proved a benefit to the country and to the blacks I shall thank God a thousand times that I was led to take my share in it.

I am placed in a position where if I were a man of great strength, I might do a great deal. But I am afraid I shall show that I am not of much account.

Extract from a letter written by Robert Gould Shaw, 1863

Source G

During the afternoon of the 18th of July last, the Fifty-fourth Massachusetts Volunteers, Col. R. G. Shaw commanding, landed upon Morris Island and reported at about 6 p.m. to Brig. Gen. G. C. Strong who informed the men of the planned assault upon Fort Wagner and asked them if they would lead it. As the dusk of evening came on, the regiment advanced at quick time, leading the column; the enemy opened upon us a brisk fire; our pace now gradually increased till it became a run. With Colonel Shaw leading, the assault was commenced. Exposed to the direct fire of canister and musketry the havoc made in our ranks was very great. Upon leaving the ditch for the parapet the men succeeded in driving the enemy from most of their guns, many following the enemy into the fort. It was here, upon the crest of the parapet, that Colonel Shaw fell. The colors [flag] of the regiment reached the crest, and were fought for by the enemy. Hand-grenades were now added to the missiles directed against the men.

The fight raged here for about an hour. When forced to abandon the fort, the men of the 54th Massachusetts formed a line about 700 yards from the fort until relieved by the Tenth Connecticut Regiment at about 2 a.m.

Report of Colonel Edward N. Hallowell, 54th Massachusetts (Colored) Infantry, 7 November 1863, on the attack on Fort Wagner

Source I

The Confederate view of the battle:

The carnage of the enemy in the confined space in front of Battery Wagner was extreme. The enemy had put the poor negroes, whom they had forced into an unnatural service, in front, to be slaughtered. The white colonel who commanded them fell, with many officers of the regiment, and the colors [flag] under which they were sent to butchery draggled in blood and sand.

Report of Brigadier-General R. S. Ripley, commanding officer of Confederate forces at Fort Wagner, 22 July 1863

A 23-year-old black sergeant called William H. Carney, who took part in the attack on Fort Wagner, reported that 'the shot – grape, canister and hand grenades – came in showers, and the columns were levelled'. The colour-bearers of the four flags carried by the 54th were also killed or wounded at this time. Sergeant Carney, though wounded and covered with blood, picked up the 'Stars and Stripes' flag of his regiment, and managed to drag it from the battlefield. For his bravery under fire, he became the first black American soldier to be awarded the Congressional Medal of Honor. Colonel Shaw and 41 other officers and men died, and 61 others were wounded in the attack. Fort Wagner remained uncaptured, but because of the bravery of the 54th Massachusetts, black soldiers played an important part in the northern war effort for the rest of the Civil War.

1 a What main differences are seen between the 'before and after' photographs of Jackson in Source B?
b Why do you think these two photographs were taken?
2 What evidence is there in this unit that black and white soldiers were not treated equally in the Union Army?
3 Tell in your own words the story of the attack on Fort Wagner.
4 Why do you think the 54th Massachusetts Volunteers were anxious to lead a successful charge on Fort Wagner?

9

Emancipation in the USA

Slavery officially came to an end in the USA during the Civil War.

How did emancipation – the freeing of the slaves – come about in America?

Black emigration

As the Civil War dragged on through 1862 without victory for the North, President Abraham Lincoln began seriously to consider emancipating the slaves. Long before becoming president, he said in a speech: 'My first impulse [upon coming to power] would be to free all the slaves, and send them back to Liberia, to their own native land.' Liberia, a colony on the west coast of Africa, was established by American abolitionists in 1822. By 1860 they had paid for the emigration of about 11,000 blacks to Liberia.

from their owners. In 1862 the slaves who had escaped from Confederate owners were declared free. Lincoln announced that he intended to make all the slaves in the southern states free from 1 January 1863. The Confederate President, Jefferson Davis, announced that northern officers captured in charge of black soldiers would be treated as criminals, and charged with encouraging 'slave revolt'. He also declared that all free blacks in the South were once again slaves.

Source A

My main purpose in this struggle is to save the Union, and is not either to save or to destroy slavery. What I do about slavery and the colored race, I do because I believe it helps to save the Union; and what I forbear [do not do], I forbear because I do not believe it would help to save the Union.

An extract from Abraham Lincoln's *Proclamation of Emancipation*, 1 January 1863

First measures

When President Lincoln decided to set the slaves free, there were still slaves in some states on the northern side such as Kentucky, Missouri, Kansas and Delaware, whose soldiers fought for the Union. Thus, the first action taken was aimed purely at slave-holders in the Confederacy, which caused a howl of outrage in the South. In 1861 all slaves used in the war against the North were taken away

Source B

Entitled 'As it was' and 'As it is', this pair of cartoons, published in the North in 1862, show the supposed effect of Northern invasion and Lincoln's plan for emancipation on Southern plantation owners and their former slaves.

Source C

A wood engraving published in Harper's Weekly on 18 March 1865 entitled: 'Marching On! – The Fifty-Fifth Massachusetts Colored Regiment singing John Brown's March in the streets of Charleston, February 21, 1865'.

In January 1865 the government finally passed the amendment to the Constitution abolishing slavery throughout the whole of the USA, but it was not until the following December that the 13th Amendment became law, and all blacks in the North and South were legally free. Meanwhile, in March 1865 the Freedmen's Bureau was established to take care of black people as they adjusted to freedom. Slaves learned of their freedom in various ways. Thousands found out by word-of-mouth, and quietly left their plantations in hopes of finding freedom behind the northern lines. Others were forced to wait until the beginning of 1866 before being liberated.

There were great celebrations as the victorious northern Army entered defeated southern cities often led by companies of black troops. Although the Civil War was at an end and the slaves had been freed, there still lay ahead many years of struggle for equality.

Source D

The arrival of the Union troops brought shouts, prayers and blessings. There were some touching incidents. A soldier riding on a mule down Meeting Street in Charleston at the head of an advancing column and bearing aloft a banner with the word 'Liberty' inscribed, was nearly unseated when a negro woman rushed up with outstretched arms, and unable to reach him in the saddle, hugged the mule, shouting 'Thank God.'

Benjamin Quarles, *The Negro in the Civil War*, 1953

---

1 What does Source A tell us about Lincoln and his attitude to black people?

2 What can we learn from Source B about the reaction of some white people to emancipation?

3 In what way do Sources C and D explain the relief felt by black people once they were emancipated?

4 Show as a time-line or diagram the main steps taken by President Lincoln in order to free the slaves.

The struggle for equality, 1865-1920

The years after the Civil War are called the 'Reconstruction'. This was a time of great disappointment. Former slaves were not given opportunities to build successful new lives.

White extremists persecuted former slaves. Some whites set up a racist secret society – the Ku Klux Klan. Klan members and other whites carried out violent attacks on many black people.

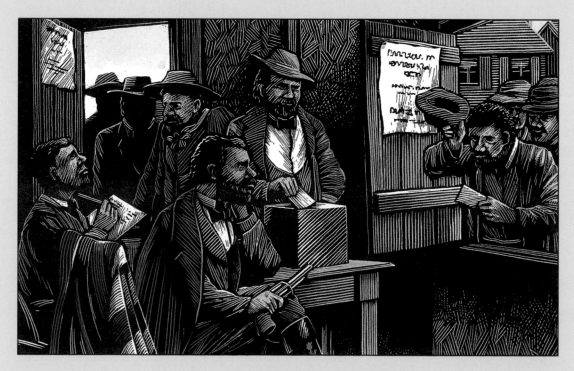

In the southern states many black men were not allowed to vote. So-called 'Jim Crow' laws were passed that discriminated against black people.

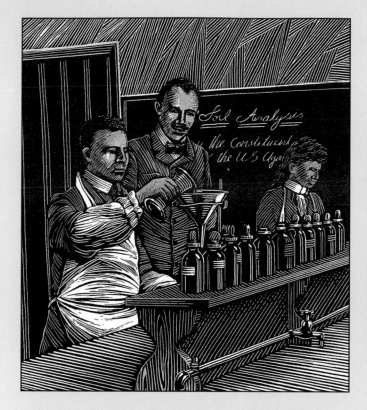

Leaders of the black community saw education as the key to progress, and as a result many black schools and colleges were founded.

Some black leaders, such as Booker T. Washington, wanted to avoid conflict with the whites. Others, such as W.E.B. DuBois, called for a tougher approach.

Around the time of the First World War, many black families left the South and moved to the North in search of jobs. Large neighbourhoods developed in cities like Chicago where black people lived in very poor conditions.

10

Reconstruction

The Civil War ended slavery but it did nothing to bring equality to the black Americans. Some white people made sure that blacks were second-class citizens.

How did black people lose out on the chance of equality?

The period after the Civil War became known as the period of Reconstruction, as the American nation had to be rebuilt. It is also known as the 'Tragic Era', as blacks in the South were not allowed to benefit fully from their emancipation or freedom. At this time a struggle began between the President – Andrew Johnson became President when Lincoln was assassinated in 1865 – who wished to reduce the newly won freedom of blacks, and politicians in Congress who wanted to see black men given civil rights and full citizenship.

Freedmen's Bureau

Black men were granted equal civil rights via the Fourteenth Amendment to the US Constitution of 1866, and the right to vote via the Fifteenth Amendment in 1870. State land in the South was opened up to black settlers, and the Freedmen's Bureau, set up in 1865, operated hospitals and schools for blacks. By 1874, approximately 20 per cent of blacks were literate.

Source B

The night school has been frequently disturbed. One evening a mob called the teacher out of the school, who on presenting himself was confronted with four revolvers, and menacing expressions of shooting him, if he did not promise to quit the place, and close the school. The freedmen promptly came to his aid, and the mob dispersed.

From a letter written in Marianna, Florida, in 1866

Source A
Freed blacks being taught in a school house.

Sharecroppers

A new agricultural system known as sharecropping was developed after the Civil War, as blacks and poor whites were allowed to work a small plot of land in return for a share of the crop. The share received by the workers was usually one third but they all had to pay their bills with the money earned. As a result they could never save enough cash to buy their own land, and often went heavily into debt.

'Black codes'

Most white southerners resented the changes introduced during Reconstruction – racial prejudice remained. They introduced strict 'black codes', or rules, which meant that blacks could not own guns, could only own property in the 'black' part of town, were not allowed to testify in court, or otherwise act as a citizen. They could be arrested for being 'impudent' to whites, or for not having a job.

The Ku Klux Klan

A secret society called the Ku Klux Klan was formed in Tennessee in December 1865 which tried to prevent blacks from gaining equal rights. Klan members claimed they believed in 'Chivalry, humanity, mercy and patriotism'. In reality it was a brutal organisation which for five years was allowed to terrorise blacks in the South through whipping, burning, raping, murdering and lynching. The Klan was outlawed in 1872, but the terror did not stop and the Klan emerged openly again in the early 20th century and is still active today in many southern states.

Source C

Black sharecroppers working on a cotton plantation, about 1870. It was coloured by painting oils over the photograph.

Source D

Ku Klux Klan violence in York County, South Carolina.

From November 1870 into September 1871 the Ku Klux Klan were out night after night raiding Negro cabins, often following a regular weekly schedule. There is no way of knowing how many persons were outraged, for as always many or most of the victims were afraid to report attacks. The best estimate is that there were 11 murders, more than 600 cases of whipping, beating, and other kinds of aggravated assault, plus uncounted instances of lesser personal abuse and threats. A few victims were white – the Klan attacked white people who were seen as helping blacks, but the vast majority were blacks, including men, women and children. In addition four or five Negro schools and churches were burned or torn down; one of them was rebuilt and destroyed four times. It was a record of sustained brutality which few places in the country ever matched.

It was after midnight when it began. On the platform stood a white robed figure. Standing or kneeling on one knee at his feet were twenty closely guarded robed men. All along the woods at the edge of the field were clubmen. The person on the platform was the Exalted Cyclops. In the centre of the great ring was an altar.

Then a dark column of men poured through a gap in the line. From a distance of three hundred feet they looked like a huddled flock of frightened herded prisoners.

The committee told us there were two thousand of them. They were lined up like soldiers at inspection. All the robed members marched in single file in and around them, putting the eyeholes in their hoods close to the faces of the men.

At the end pledges were read to them which they swore to with their right hands on their hearts and their left hands uplifted. Those who followed the pledges noted that they emphasised white supremacy to combat in all things the Negro, the Catholic, the Jew, and the foreign-born generally. At the end of the prayer the great cross was lighted and blazed up so that it could be seen seven miles away.

A newspaper report about a meeting of the Ku Klux Klan, 3 May 1923

The Granger Collection, New York

Source F

A contemporary coloured engraving of two captured Ku Klux Klan members in Huntsville, Alabama, in 1868.

Lynching

Blacks in the South continued to be terrorised by white violence even after the Ku Klux Klan was outlawed. Lynching was the most horrifying type of terrorism, when black people accused of crimes (or sometimes not accused of anything) were dragged to a tree and hanged. Often white police would do little or nothing to stop these dreadful events from happening. In 1892, a typical year, a total of 161 blacks were lynched.

Source G

A lynching in 1935.

Blacks lose their voting rights

The end of the Ku Klux Klan terror in 1872 did not prevent blacks from losing many of their newly won rights. The US government was reluctant to support black people, and was more interested in winning the support of white southerners. Many black men were disqualified from voting and those who tried were terrorised into not voting. A poll tax was introduced which most poor blacks could not afford to pay. Failure to pay meant they could not vote. The 'grandfather clause' ordered that men whose grandfathers had been slaves lost their right to vote. A literacy test required voters to explain the meaning of a legal document. Low reading skills therefore prevented many poorly educated blacks from qualifying to vote.

'Jim Crow' laws

Between the years 1890 and 1910, a series of 'Jim Crow' laws were passed by the state governments in the South which discriminated against blacks and encouraged segregation, or separate and unequal treatment. Named after a song called *Jump Jim Crow*, composed in 1828 by white comedian, Thomas Rice, which made fun of black people, these laws prevented blacks from using the same public facilities as whites, and ensured that they were treated as second-class citizens. In 1896 a black man named Homer Plessey challenged a Louisiana railroad company because he was made to sit in a 'colored only' carriage. The US Supreme Court agreed with the railroad company, and said that segregated, or separate, public facilities for blacks and whites were legal. This ruling was to stand as the law in the United States until 1954. The decision was disastrous for black Americans because it encouraged the white South to introduce many more 'Jim Crow' laws. (Although it was not a matter of law, the same sort of discrimination was also common in the North.) Marriage between black and white people became illegal in some states. Separate black-only residential areas were established in less desirable parts of most southern cities and towns. Black citizens were prevented from using the same restaurants, hotels and theatres as whites. Segregation in the armed services, begun in the US Army during the Civil War, became the norm.

Source H

A segregated drinking fountain being used in the American South.

---

1 Explain in your own words how blacks were denied their civil rights and liberties in each of the following areas :

   a sharecropping

   b black codes

   c the Ku Klux Klan

   d voting rights

2 What do lynching and the activities of the Ku Klux Klan tell us about the attitudes of some white people in the years after the war?

11

Pioneers, cowboys and buffalo soldiers

Thousands of films celebrate the story of the American West.
Almost all of these films ignore the contribution
of black Americans.

What part did black people play in this aspect of American history?

Pioneers

Black people were involved in the earliest exploration
and settlement of the North American West. Estevanico,
or 'Little Stephen', a Spanish slave from the west coast of
Morocco, landed on the Texas coast in 1528, and was
captured with his master by Indians. After seven years in
captivity, they escaped to New Spain, or Mexico, where
their stories of the Seven Cities of Cibola were directly
responsible for further expeditions to Texas. In 1781,
blacks and black/Indian families helped to found what is
now the largest city in the West – Los Angeles. A black
slave named York took part in the famous Lewis and
Clark expedition of 1804–6, which explored North
America from the Mississippi River to the Pacific Ocean.

Some runaway slaves joined forces with native
Americans. A US Army survey of the Choctaw nation in
1831 showed that the tribe included 512 blacks. The
Pamunkey tribe of Virginia included so many blacks that
whites petitioned the government to take their land
away. The Shawnees and the Cherokees used their
villages as hiding places for runaway slaves heading for
Canada.

Source A

In the 1790s white missionaries, sent to convert the Delaware tribe to Christianity before their removal to the Far West, entered this report into the church records:

They could not help remembering that we had a people among us, whom, because they differed from us in colour, we had made slaves of, and made them suffer great hardships, and lead miserable lives. Now they could not see any reason, if a people being black entitled us thus to deal with them, why a red colour should not equally justify the same treatment. They therefore determined to wait, to see whether all the black people amongst us were made thus happy and joyful before they would put confidence in our promises: for they thought a people who had suffered so much and so long by our means, should be entitled to our first attention; and therefore they had sent back the two missionaries, with many thanks, promising that when they saw the black people among us restored to freedom and happiness they would gladly receive our missionaries.

Cowboys

The Hollywood version of the past largely ignores the large numbers of black cowboys. More than 5,000 blacks played a part in the early cattle drives from Texas to Missouri. Many of the first black cowboys were slaves brought by their masters from the southern states.

Others found their way West as runaways or freedmen. One of the best known black cowboys was Tennessee-born Nat Love, who came east to Kansas as a freedman in 1869. It is said that he asked for a job with the Duval 'outfit' of Texas, who were going home after a cattle drive. He was given the roughest horse to ride in order to prove himself, and was able to stay in the saddle and got the job. In 1876 he won prizes at Deadwood, South Dakota, for roping wild horses and target shooting. He was given the nickname 'Deadwood Dick' as champion roper of the West.

Source B

Nat Love, the black cowboy who became famous as 'Deadwood Dick', photographed in the 1870s.

Source C

I thought I had rode pitching horses before, but from the time I mounted old Good Eye I knew I had not learned what pitching was. This proved the worst horse to ride I had ever mounted in my life, but I stayed with him and the cowboys were the most surprised outfit you ever saw, as they had taken me for a tenderfoot, pure and simple. After the horse got tired and I dismounted the boss said he would give me a job and pay me $30.00 per month.

The Life and Adventures of Nat Love, by himself, 1907

Source D

They rode with white Texans, Mexicans and Indians. All the real cowboys – black, brown, red and white – shared the same jobs and dangers. They ate the same food and slept on the same ground; but when the long drives ended and the great plains were tamed and fenced, the trails ended too. The cattle were fenced in, and Negroes fenced out.

P. Durham and E. L. Jones, *The Negro Cowboys*, 1965

Buffalo soldiers

Twenty per cent of the soldiers who fought against the native peoples of North America were blacks. The Congressional Act of 28 July 1866 created four segregated black regiments, the 24th and 25th Infantry, and the 9th and 10th Cavalry. Called 'buffalo soldiers' by the Indians, black cavalrymen fought in almost every part of the West from Mexico to Montana. Led at first by white officers, the first black officer, Henry Flipper, graduated from the military academy at West Point, New York, in 1877, and joined the 10th Cavalry during the same year. Blacks also served as scouts and interpreters with white regiments.

Source F
A black trooper talking with a native American in sign language.

Source E
Second Lieutenant Henry Flipper, the first black officer to graduate from West Point Military Academy.

1 What information can you find in this unit to suggest that black Americans played an important role in:

   a exploring America

   b the work of the cowboys

   c the activities of the US Army during the Indian Wars

   d the life of the Indian tribes?

2 Hollywood film-makers have made movies about each of the topics mentioned in question 1. Black people have not featured very much in these films. Why do you think this is?

Source G

Captain Dodge's Colored Troops to the rescue. *The 9th Cavalry had a reputation for arriving just in the nick of time to rescue settlers or other soldiers, but they have never appeared in any cowboy movie of the Old West.*

Source H

In 1889, a small detachment of black soldiers of the 24th Infantry and 9th Cavalry crossed the plains from Fort Grant to Fort Thomas guarding the army paymaster and his strong-box. A large gang of outlaws had placed a boulder in their path and waited in ambush. The paymaster describes what happened when the soldiers investigated the boulder blocking the road.

They were nearly all at the boulder when a signal shot was fired from the ledge of rocks about fifty feet above to the right, which was instantly followed by a volley, believed by myself and the entire party, to be fifteen or twenty shots.

A sharp, short fight, lasting something over thirty minutes, ensued during which time the officers and privates, eight of whom were wounded, two being shot twice, behaved in the most courageous and heroic manner.

Sergeant Brown, though shot through the abdomen did not quit the field until again wounded, this time through the arm. Private Burge who was to my immediate right, received a bad wound in the hand, but gallantly held his post, resting his rifle on his fore-arm and continuing to fire with much coolness, until shot through the thigh and twice through the hat. Private Arrington was shot through the shoulder, while fighting from this same position. Private Hams, Wheeler, and Harrison were also wounded, to my immediate left, while bravely doing their duty under a murderous cross-fire.

The brigands [outlaws] fought from six well-constructed, stone forts; the arrangements seemed thorough, the surprise complete.

I was a soldier in General Grant's old regiment, and during the entire Civil War it was justly proud of its record of sixteen battles but I never witnessed better courage or better fighting than shown by these colored soldiers, on May 11, 1889.

J. W. Wham, a soldier in the US Army, 1889

12

Early black protest

By the beginning of the 20th century, black people had seen their hopes and dreams of equality fading away. New black leaders emerged to attempt to deal with the situation confronting black people.

Who were these new leaders of America's black people? What were their aims and what did they achieve?

Ida B. Wells

Born a slave, Ida B. Wells became one of the most active black women in the struggle for racial equality, and devoted her life to the fight against lynching and discrimination. She became a journalist, a leading member of the National Association of Colored Women, and a founder member of the National Association for the Advancement of Colored People, or NAACP.

At 14 years of age, Ida B. Wells was orphaned and had to bring up four younger brothers and sisters. Despite this she kept on with her education and put herself through college. She started her campaign against lynching in Tennessee at the age of 19. Her articles in the Memphis *Free Speech* exposed the growing number of lynchings. In 1892 she published information showing that the lynching of three successful black grocers was the work of their white competitors. The press was wrecked and she was driven from Memphis but she carried her crusade to northern cities and to Europe. In 1898 she led a delegation of women and Congressmen to President William F. McKinley to protest against lynching. Nothing was done but she continued her campaign until her death in 1931.

Source A

Ida B. Wells wrote this in a book which revealed the truth about the widespread lynching of black people:

If it were known that cannibals had burned three human beings alive in the past two years, the whole of Christendom would be roused to devise ways to put a stop to it. Can you remain silent and inactive when such things [as lynchings] are done in our own community and country?

Booker T. Washington

Booker T. Washington was born into slavery in Virginia in 1856. After struggling to gain an education, he became a teacher and in 1881 opened the Tuskegee Institute in Alabama, where black youths received education and industrial training. This school received backing from wealthy white people and, although not an academic institution, it developed into one of the best schools for black people in the South.

Washington encouraged black people to avoid conflict with whites despite the growing number of 'Jim Crow' laws and lynchings. He believed it was possible for blacks to remain separate from whites, but wished to see them co-operate in the world of work. This view – the acceptance of segregation – became known as the 'Atlanta Compromise', and was welcomed by many white people.

Source B

In my opinion, the Negro should seek constantly in every manly, straight-forward manner to make friends of the white man by whose side he lives.

Part of a speech made by Booker T. Washington in Atlanta, Georgia, in 1895

W. E. B. DuBois

W. E. B. DuBois was born in Massachusetts in 1868. A brilliant student, he was the first black person to receive a doctorate degree at Harvard, one of the top universities in the USA. DuBois disagreed with Booker T. Washington's views on race relations, and encouraged black people to band together and fight for their rights.

In 1905 W. E. B. DuBois and about 30 other black leaders met at Niagara Falls, where they founded the Niagara Movement which in 1910 expanded into the National Association for the Advancement of Colored People. The NAACP became the main organisation fighting for civil rights, equal job opportunities, education, and the right to vote for black people. Its message was more radical than that of Booker T. Washington. Branches of this organisation were established in all major cities in the United States.

Source C

Some people in Chicago, Philadelphia, Atlantic City, Columbus in Ohio, and other northern cities are quietly trying to establish separate colored schools. This is wrong, and should be resisted by black men and white.

W. E. B. DuBois, November 1910

Marcus Garvey

Jamaican-born Marcus Garvey encouraged the black people of the Americas to return to Africa in order to create a new and powerful black African nation. He founded the Universal Negro Improvement Association in the United States in 1916, which within two years had 1,120 branches in 40 countries. Of a new black African empire, he said: 'It is in the wind. It is coming. One day, like a storm, it will be here.'

Marcus Garvey had moved to the USA during the First World War. From his headquarters in Harlem in New York, Garvey declared himself the 'Leader of the Negro Peoples of the World', and using slogans such as 'Black is beautiful', he encouraged blacks to take pride in their race and to stand up for their rights. He set up the Black Star Shipping Line in order to take black people 'home'. His dream was never realised. The land he hoped to buy in Liberia was sold to an American company, and he was found guilty of fraud. Although he protested his innocence, he was imprisoned for two years, after which he received a pardon, and was sent back to Jamaica. Garvey died in London in 1940.

Source D

This is how Marcus Garvey explained his beliefs to white Americans in 1923:

Why should the Negro die? Has he not served America and the world? Has he not borne the burden of civilization in this Western world for three hundred years? Has he not contributed his best to America? Surely all this stands to his credit, but there will not be enough room and the one answer is 'find a place.' We have found a place, it is Africa and as black men for three centuries have helped white men build America, surely generous and grateful white men will help black men build Africa.

Despite the work of these and other black leaders, the black people of the United States continued to be denied the rights which had been called for by the NAACP in 1905. Between 1890 and 1920 approximately 300,000 blacks migrated from the South to the industrial cities of the North, or West to California, in hopes of escaping the 'Jim Crow' laws, poverty and the constant threat of lynching. There they found almost as much prejudice and racism as in the South. The First World War provided an opportunity for many blacks to find employment in industry, but they were often the first to lose their jobs when white soldiers returned.

Source E

Some of the 200,000 black soldiers who served in the United States Army during the First World War, fought between 1914 and 1918. The 371st Infantry Regiment won 121 French Croix de Guerre and 27 American Distinguished Service Crosses.

Source F

An account of the reception black American soldiers received on their return to the USA after the First World War:

A fearful wave of lynchings and anti-Negro violence swept the nation. Ignorant, hate-filled whites, afraid that these returned Negro soldiers would insist on fair treatment as men and as citizens, decided that now was the time 'to keep them from stepping out of their place.' Discharged Negro soldiers, some still in uniform, were among the victims of these rampaging white mobs.

W. L. Katz, *Eyewitness: the Negro in American History*, 1974

1 Explain the importance of Ida B. Wells in the black struggle for equality.

2 Booker T. Washington, W. E. B. DuBois and Marcus Garvey all wanted equality for black people in the USA, yet they had different ideas on how this should be achieved. Describe how their ideas differ.

3 Booker T. Washington was liked by some white leaders but many of them were opposed to the methods W. E. B. DuBois and Marcus Garvey used to gain equality for blacks. Why do you think this was?

4 Look at Sources E and F.

a What happened when black soldiers returned from the war in Europe?

b How do you think black soldiers felt at this treatment?

13

Civil rights since the 1920s

The 20th century has seen many developments in black American history. One of the most dramatic periods came in the 1950s and 1960s with the rise of the Civil Rights movement and its leader, Martin Luther King.

What impact did the Civil Rights movement have on the lives of black Americans?

Between 1915 and 1930 many black families left the southern countryside to find jobs in the cities of the North. Most of them lived in separate black neighbourhoods. Although at first there were jobs in the factories, black people could only get badly paid unskilled work. During the Depression of the 1930s many of these jobs disappeared and there was a high level of unemployment and poverty.

Black people in the South continued to be treated with vicious racism. A famous law case that symbolised this racism took place in Scottsboro, Alabama in 1931. Two white women accused nine young black men of rape. The white jury believed the women. (One of the women later confessed that she had been lying.) Eight of the black men were sentenced to death. The United States Supreme Court stopped the state of Alabama from executing the men but they remained in jail for many years.

The Second World War marked an important turning point for black Americans. They volunteered in large numbers to join the armed services. Racism was built into the American military system and black people served in segregated black units. According to the government the war was fought to defend freedom in Europe and the wider world. To many black people this appeared hypocritical because they did not have full freedom at home.

The war did not put a stop to white violence against black people. When black soldiers returned home at the end of the war there was a new upsurge of lynching in the South.

Source A

A modern black writer reflects on the impact of the war:

In a memorable 1941 speech President Roosevelt had opened up a vision of a world in which everyone would enjoy freedom of expression, freedom of worship, freedom from want and freedom from fear. These four freedoms were later adopted as the war aims of the Allies. Yet blacks could not help noticing the discrepancy between the resounding wartime slogans and their own condition.

Richard Long, *Black Americana*, 1985

Source B

The famous actor, Paul Robeson, visited President Truman in 1946 and demanded a new federal law to stamp out lynching. The request was refused:

I stand here ashamed. Ashamed that it is necessary – 84 years after the Emancipation Proclamation – to publicly expose and fight the horrible contradiction that renders hollow our promises to lead the people of the world to freedom.

Paul Robeson, 1946

After the war there was a renewed determination among black people to win a fair deal. The struggle for equality in the 1950s and 1960s became known as the Civil Rights movement. The greatest leader of the black community during these years was a clergyman called Martin Luther King. King and his followers called for an end to segregation: the separate and inferior treatment of black people. The Civil Rights campaign began in 1955, when a woman called Rosa Parkes from Montgomery, Alabama, refused to give up her seat on a bus to a white man. She was arrested for this. In response, King helped to organise a boycott by local black people of the bus company.

The Montgomery bus boycott was the first of many. King believed in non-violent direct action. In the late 1950s young black demonstrators organised boycotts and demonstrations across the southern states. Protesters staged 'sit-ins' – they would not leave when refused service at white-only restaurants. In 1961 they carried out a famous 'freedom ride' from Washington to New Orleans. The freedom riders travelled on a series of public buses and on each one they insisted on sitting in the 'whites only' section.

One important aspect of the Civil Rights movement was the fight for mixed schools. The black pressure group, the National Association for the Advancement of Colored People, demanded an end to segregated schools. In 1954, the US Supreme Court declared such schools to be illegal. White local politicians in the South fought against mixed schooling and it was not until the 1960s that schools in most southern states accepted both black and white pupils. There was a famous conflict in 1957 at Little Rock, Arkansas, when the state governor refused to let black students into Little Rock High School. Amid lynching threats against the black students, the US President intervened and the pupils were escorted into school under the protection of federal troops.

Source C

Martin Luther King spoke to a large meeting on the first day of the bus boycott:

There comes a time when people get tired. We are tired – tired of being segregated and humiliated, tired of being kicked about by the brutal feet of oppression. If you will protest courageously and yet with dignity and Christian love historians will say, 'There lived a great people – a black people – who injected a new meaning and dignity into the veins of civilisation'.

Martin Luther King, 1955

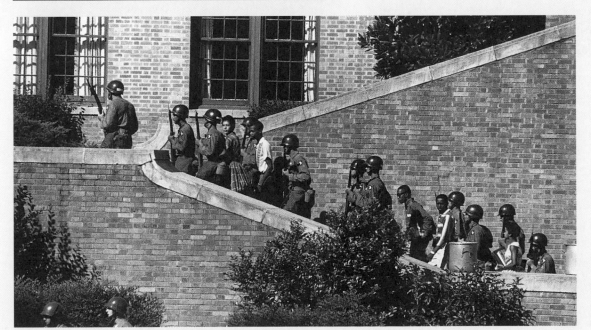

Source D

High school pupils escorted into Little Rock High School by federal troops, 1957.

The Civil Rights movement led to the end of much segregation in the South. Martin Luther King found it more difficult to get the government to bring in a law making racial discrimination illegal. In 1963 a demonstration of about half a million people took place in Washington calling for a law against discrimination. King was a brilliant public speaker and it was at this demonstration that he made one of his most famous speeches.

As a result of the pressure from King and other Civil Rights activists, the American government finally agreed to change the law. The Civil Rights Act of 1964 made racial discrimination illegal. The Voting Rights Act of 1965 extended equal voting rights for black and white people to the southern states. King's own contribution was recognised in 1964 when he won the Nobel Peace Prize.

However, not all black people supported Martin Luther King – some disagreed with his non-violent approach. The most influential militant black leader was known as 'Malcolm X'. He was assassinated in 1965.

Source E

Martin Luther King, speaking at a massive rally in Washington gave one of the most memorable speeches of the century:

I have a dream that one day even the state of Mississippi will be transformed into an oasis of peace and justice. I have a dream that one day my four little children will live in a nation where they will not be judged by the color of their skin. When we allow freedom to ring from every town and every hamlet, from every state and every city, we will be able to speed up the day when all God's children, black and white, Jews and gentiles, Protestants and Catholics, will be able to join hands and sing in the words of the old Negro spiritual, 'Free at last! Free at last! Great God Almighty, we are free at last!'

Martin Luther King, 1963

Source F

Malcolm X was not pleased when Martin Luther King was given the Nobel Peace Prize:

He got the peace prize, we got the problem. I don't want the white man to give me medals. If I'm following a general and he's leading me into battle, and the enemy tend to give him rewards, I get suspicious of him.

Malcolm X, 1964

The achievements of the Civil Rights movement did not end the poverty and unequal treatment of many black people. Between 1965 and 1969 there was widespread violent rioting in the black neighbourhoods of cities in the West and the North. Some young black people rejected the message of King; they were known as the 'Black Power' movement.

At the age of 39, Martin Luther King was shot dead in 1968. His killer was a white racist. Since his death there have been many achievements and many difficulties for black Americans. King's dream of a harmonious multi-racial America is still far from a reality. Individual black Americans have enjoyed extremely successful careers in many fields. However, racism and inequality remain. By the early 1990s the average black family had little more than half the income of the average white family. Black anger was seen in 1992 when rioting spread through the black neighbourhoods of Los Angeles. The spark for this explosion was the fact that four white police officers were filmed brutally assaulting a black motorist, Rodney King, but were not punished in the courts.

Source G

Two black American sprinters, Tommy Smith and John Carlos, raised their fists in the Black Power salute as they received their medals at the 1968 Olympics.

Source H

This writer was a leading figure in the Black Power movement:

After years we are almost at the same point – because we demonstrated from a point of weakness. We cannot be expected any longer to march and have our heads broken in order to say to whites: 'Come on, you're nice guys'. For you are not nice guys. We have found you out. We have to work

Source I *Rodney King appealing for an end to the riots in Los Angeles, 1 May 1992.*

Imagine that you have been commissioned to make a radio documentary about the life of Martin Luther King. Write the script of the documentary mentioning:
- the background of racism and inequality
- King's achievements and assassination
- critics of King's approach
- the experience of black Americans since his death.

Index